HOW TO MAKE £25K - £100K

IN YOUR OWN

VENTURE CAPITAL BUSINESS

By Ray Fox, B.SC., FCIS, Principal, The Bottom Line Consultancy

Copyright Estelle-Alan Publications © 1996

First Edition published in 2015 by The Bottom Line Consultancy
Hurst Cottage, Bottle Square Lane, Radnage,
Buckinghamshire. HP14 4DP, United Kingdom
Tel: 01494 483728 Fax: 01494 484039
Email: fox@estelle-alan.com

Ray Fox has asserted his right to be identified as the author of this work in accordance with sections 77 and 78 of the Copyright, Designs and Patents Act 1988.

ISBN-13: 978-1514624883
ISBN-10: 1514624885

First edition 2015
Printed and bound by Amazon Creates
NOTE: The material contained in this book is set out in good faith for general guidance and no liability can be accepted for loss or expense incurred as a result of relying in particular circumstances on statements made in this book. Laws and regulations are complex and liable to change, and readers should check the current positions with the relevant authorities in their country of origin before making personal arrangements.

This book is available online and at all good bookstores.

Contents Page

PART 1

Introduction

The business world of the 21st Century can be very strange. All over the world there are literally tens of thousands of individuals and companies who are desperate for a cash injection - this could be for a new factory, an acquisition, a Management-Buy-Out (MBO), a Management-Buy-In (MBI), to purchase a new retail unit or for a myriad of other reasons. The thing which is particularly strange, is that there are similarly tens of thousands of companies, individuals and organisations who have cash that they wish to invest but can't find a safe and profitable project in which to invest their funds. In the UK, there a number of well known Venture Capital providers such as CinVen [www.cinven.com] and Investors in Industry [www.3i.com].

For the average seeker of funds, the only place they would consider approaching are the High Street Banks. As we all know, the High Street Banks don't want to lend money to those who need it for what might be called speculative ventures. They only want to lend money to rock solid organisations where there are absolutely no risks involved. However, a Venture Capital provider is prepared to offer funds for a slightly more risky investment in the knowledge that the loan will provide a higher than normal return. It may also provide the Investor with an equity interest as well as the possibility that the organisation may float on a public stock exchange providing the Investor with the potential of a spectacular financial gain.

So, here is an interesting question. If there are large numbers of organisations looking for funds and a large number of potential investors who are looking for an investment, why don't the two types of parties get together? Quite simply, the two groups, in general, don't know how to get in touch with one another. This is where the Venture Capital Consultant can make a substantial commission - by introducing one party to the other and thereby earning a significant fee for their trouble. Not only can you earn substantial fees and commissions, but the Venture Capital business you are about to set up is _your_ business - you will own it, you will run it, you will have unlimited potential with little or no r sk, little or no capital outlay and no boss looking over your shoulder telling you how to run your business.

The financial potential is immense. Let us consider the XYZ trading company. They wish to borrow £1M to buy a small competitor. They ask you to assist them. They pay you a consultancy fee of £2,000 to write a professional business plan (we will show you how to do it - or you could ask a firm of accountants to do it for you). They will pay you an advance against your expenses of £1,000 to enable you to identify potential investors. When an offer is made, you will charge them 1% of the project amount (i.e. £10,000). The investor will ask for certain conditions to be met e.g. a particular rate of return, an equity interest etc. Once the negotiations are concluded and the funds are transferred, you can charge a second fee for conclusion - usually the same as the offer fee i.e. £10,000. One deal and you have made in excess of £20,000. How many of these do you have to handle before you can give up your full time job and run your Venture Capital Consultancy full time?

Getting Started

It is extremely easy to set up your own Venture Capital business. The following will show you how easy it is.

In this business you are your own boss. You work when you like for as long as you like. When you first start your business, you will probably be running it part-time. This is not a problem - you can run the business during the day, in the evenings or at weekends.

A knowledge of foreign languages is not necessary. Although you will probably receive overseas enquiries, English is the language of international business and by far the majority of companies in almost every country of the world speak English.

Another advantage of this type of business is that you require little or no capital expenditure. A functional computer with internet access, printer, a desk, a chair and a small amount of filing space and you are in business. You do not need expensive offices with 21st Century electronic facilities. When the business begins to grow, you may be inclined to purchase these but at the beginning your primary expenses are paper, business cards, postage, telephone calls, broadband and the occasional advertisement. Similarly, you will not require any expensive staff to employ. You can run the business by yourself (or with your spouse) but you will not need to employ anybody, unless of course, you wish to.

Another advantage is that you will not be buying any stock of products and so tying up any of your precious capital or which requires a large storage area. Neither will you require any specialised knowledge of your Clients' products.

Once you begin your business, you will realise that there is no shortage of organisations who require capital. Surprisingly, once you become well known in the Venture Capital environment, you will find that there is similarly no shortage of potential investors. Consequently, it is up to you how many deals you handle and your earnings will be limited only by the amount of time you wish to spend making money. How many businesses can offer you the same as that?

Your Office

You do not need expensive or elaborate office space to start up your business. If need be, you could start off by running your business from the kitchen, dining room table or from a spare bedroom. Wherever you can work quietly, where you will not be disturbed, nor disturb others, is good enough.

The basic requirements have already been mentioned above. If these are not readily available, the small ads in your local newspaper will invariably lead you to inexpensive second - hand equipment at reasonable prices.

Your Trading Image

The first thing to consider here is your trading style. Your image to the outside world is critical to your future prosperity. Calling yourself something like "Joe Bloggs" is not likely to fire the imagination. Using a name like "Joe Bloggs Venture Capital", "Joe Bloggs Commercial Funding", "JB International Enterprises" or "The JB Mortgage Consultancy" certainly creates the right impression. As an alternative, you could form a limited company which you would be a Director of. Companies House (www.companieshouse.gov.uk) can send you the necessary information although it is possible to buy a limited company off the shelf. Any Accountant or Lawyer can assist you here and the Company could be formed within days for around £100. Don't forget to contact your Bank to open a business bank account. As with all business matters, it is very important to keep your personal financial affairs separate from your business financial affairs.

As mentioned above, your image is all important. As the old expression goes, you don't get a second chance of a first impression. Consequently, you should invest in quality letter-headed paper, matching envelopes and business cards. Unless you have contacts with a good printer, you should visit one of the major High Street printing franchises such as PDC Copyprint or Pronto Print who will do this for you quickly and inexpensively. Alternatively, you can contact The Printing Works (for details see Part 2) who are specialists in this form of printing. However, modern printers are so efficient that you can even print your letter headed paper and business cards yourself. Staples supplies a range of DECadry paper that is designed for an individual to print their own business cards as well as quality Conqueror paper for letter heads.

How to find Clients to represent

There are a number of methods to find organisations who are looking for Commercial Finance or Venture Capital funds. The most common is by advertising. A sure way of knowing where to advertise and to have the confidence that advertising works, is to look in the business section of the major newspapers. In Part 3 is a selection of previous advertisements that have worked for other advertisers.

An alternative method to identify potential Clients is Direct Mail. Many organisations can help you with Direct Mail and they can provide lists of Managing Directors, Finance Directors etc on sticky self adhesive labels. All you need to do is to peel off the label and affix them to an envelope. Enclose in the envelope a mailshot which summarises the service you are offering (see Part 3 for an example) and post them. Mailing lists cost about £75 - £100 for a thousand labels. In most cases, you only have the right to use the names and addresses once but if you send out a few thousand, the total cost will only be a couple of hundred pounds and I am certain you will get a positive response. As with all things, you will need to try different styles and approaches to see which suits you best and gets you the best response.

It is also possible to buy email addresses of such organisations and there are a number of groups on Linked-In [www.Linkedin.com] that specialise in finance.

Confidentiality

Once you have met your potential Client and discussed his requirements, it is often the case that the Client will ask you to keep confidential the details he is about to give you. For example, the Client may have an invention which he wants to protect or he may be about to launch a take-over bid and wants the details kept confidential. Whatever the reasons, in general there are no reasons for you not to sign a Confidentiality Agreement and a sample is enclosed in Part 3. Remember, you must comply with the terms of the Confidentiality Agreement or your Client may sue you.

The Business Plan

Without doubt, the business plan is one of the most critical areas in the whole exercise. It has a number of primary functions. Firstly, it helps the Client to crystallise and focus their ideas, set objectives and monitor their performance. It is, secondly, the fundamental document to be used as a vehicle for attracting external finance. From your perspective, the business plan has an added advantage as you can charge the Client for producing it. Most Consultants work on a time basis to produce a business plan which could take, say, three days work or more to produce. Many Consultants charge £500 - £750 per day for this type of work. If you are not comfortable in producing the business plan, there are accountants and law firms who will be happy to produce it for your Client. If you decide to produce the business plan yourself, I can do no better than recommend an excellent book published by the BVCA [www.bvca.co.uk] in conjunction with a major Accountancy firm called "Business Plans and Financing Proposals" which is available from the BVCA.

Fee structures

Obviously, you are not going to put in a lot of effort to secure funds for your Client unless you have a clear understanding of the fees you are going to charge. As a medium through which potential investors are put in touch with Clients seeking funds, there are many methods of charging for your time and effort. As I have already intimated, these fall into 4 categories.

a. Business Plan Fee

As I have already mentioned, you can charge a fee for the production of the Business Plan. This is invariably based on a time basis i.e. so many days at £X per day. Some Consultants choose to work on a fixed fee basis e.g. £1,500 for the complete plan regardless of how long it takes. You will need to decide which suits you best.

b. Up front fees against expenses

Once you commence your search for funds, you will be incurring expenses. These could be for advertising, meeting potential investors, etc. These should be agreed in advance with your Client. For example, your expense allocation could be 0.1% (i.e. one tenth of one per-cent) of the funds requested subject to a minimum of say £1,500. For example, suppose your Client is looking for £2,500,000. You will charge £2,500 expenses. In many cases, this expenses fee will be deducted from the fee you charge "on-offer" - see 3 below.

c. Offer fees

Once you have placed advertisements for the funds, in addition to the cost of the adverts, you will probably have meetings to attend and negotiations to thrash out an equitable offer. This offer can take many forms. Some investors will simply want a rate of return on their investment higher than they can get by putting their money on the Stock Exchange or on long term deposit with a Bank or Building Society. For example, if a Bank were paying, say, 5% in a deposit account, an investor who was putting money into what might be considered a risky form of investment might ask for a 20% return or even higher. They may ask for some form of security or collateral e.g. against your Clients' business or house. They may ask for an equity interest in your Clients' business or they could ask for an appointment as a Non-Executive Director of your Clients' business to oversee their investment. If they are looking to appoint a Non-Executive Director, you should take a look at www.NEDexchange.co.uk and www.ProfessionalDirectors.co.uk who will be able to find a Non-Executive Director for your Client.

Whatever form the offer takes, you have completed the next part of your assignment which was to secure an offer. This entitles you to charge your Client additional fees at the pre-agreed rate. Some Consultants will charge a fee as a percentage of the funds obtained. This could vary from 1% - 3% of the funds. So for example, if you obtained an offer for £2,500,000 and you had agreed a fee of 1½%, you would be entitled to a fee of £37,500. As mentioned above, many Venture Capital Consultants deduct the "up front fees against expenses" amount. In this example, you would invoice the Client for £35,000 (i.e. £37,500 less

14

£2,500). But this is not the end of matters. Having got an offer made, you now need to proceed to completion.

d. Completion

There is still a lot of work to be done. Although you have achieved one of your major objectives in securing an offer of funds, your Client may be unhappy with the details of the offer. It will now be up to you to thrash out an amicable settlement between the various parties. This may involve you in time consuming negotiations and meetings between the various parties. Legal documents will need to be drawn up and you will act as the go-between in all these discussions. This part could take weeks, if not months, before the actual funds are transferred to your Client. On completion, you will be entitled to another tranche of fees which, again, can vary from 1% - 3% of the amount of the funds being transferred. Let's say you agree a 1% fee for completion, which would entitle you to an additional £25,000. In total you would have earned £60,000 in fees plus the cost of the business plan. Not bad for one deal!!

A couple of points to remember here. Always get your fees agreed up front with your Client *before* you commence the project. Once the Client has the funds he needs, it is easy for him to forget the amount of time and energy you had invested to secure the money. Make sure you are paid for each stage before you commence work on the next stage. On completion, try and ensure that the investor pays you your fees from the amount being paid to your Client before the funds are actually transferred. As in the example above, your Client is about to receive £2,500,000 from an investor. Your fee is £25,000. Get the investor to pay your Client £2,475,000 and your fee of £25,000 direct to you. This will eliminate any risks for you. If you have any doubts about being paid, invest a few hundred pounds in a local lawyer to draw up a document of appointment outlining what fees you can charge and when. Get this agreement signed by your Client before you commence work.

How to find the funds for your Clients

As with other aspects of Venture Capital, advertising is usually the most successful. Many of the major business papers both in the UK and from around the world carry advertising for investors who wish to invest money. However the two most commonly used vehicles are VCR and BVCA. Phone numbers and addresses for these organisations are included in Part 2.

The Gazette is a simple and cost effective market place through which to make contact with potential investment partners. At the time of writing, the annual subscription to The Gazette is only £75 and provides an enormous number of contacts in the Venture capital world. As an example, I have enclosed in Part 3, a copy from a previous issue which lists three pages of Banks and Building Societies who specialise in Venture Capital with names and addresses for you to contact. I would seriously recommend that you subscribe to The Gazette. It is also one of the most effective mediums through which to advertise for funds. Another benefit of The Gazette is that once you register, you can apply to become one of their "Principal Advisors", and, if successful, you might receive leads direct from the magazine publishers.

VCR is very similar to The Gazette. To quote from its own literature, "VCR is the leading national Business Angel introduction Agency, directly linking private investors and small business..............VCR publishes a monthly Report which features details of small businesses seeking equity capital (£20,000 - £2M) and is subscribed to by a network of private investors. Investors......subscribe annually to VCR to receive a regular flow of......investment opportunities". VCR also publish a Directory called

"The VCR Guide to Venture Capital in the UK + Europe". It also lists over 1,000 sources of Venture Capital both in the UK and Europe. Details of this Directory are included in Part 3.

BVCA represents most major sources of Venture Capital in the UK. BVCA members are active in making long term equity investments, primarily in unquoted companies. By telephoning BVCA, you can obtain a free of charge directory of members. This will include a list of over 100 organisations who all have funds to invest in projects such as those that your Client is seeking funds for. In addition, the Directory includes Financial and Professional Organisations who have an interest in investing in Venture Capital projects. BVCA can also put you in touch with their European counterpart (See Part 2 for address and telephone number) if you wish to handle enquiries outside of the UK.

Further tips

You now have everything you need to know to set up and run a successful Venture Capital business. There are a couple of other things you will need to be aware of.

1. Make sure you keep proper books of account. Get the name of a local accountant from the Yellow Pages or Thomson Directory. He can advise you how to keep your records so as to minimise your tax liability and maximise your profits. It may be worth investing in a computerised accounting software page, such as Quickbooks. This is available from Currys PC World

2. You will probably need to register for VAT. Again, your accountant can advise you.

3. Don't get excited too quickly. Some of the numbers we have quoted here can only be charged when you have a successful business operating with a dozen projects on the go at any one time. At the beginning don't get too greedy. There is a lot of competition out there and you mustn't charge yourself out of the running. Do some homework on the fees that other organisations charge. Send them a letter or email asking them for information about their services and then you can get a better idea of the fees they actually charge. (See part 3 for an example) Offer lower rates than they do - say 0.75% on offer and 0.75% on completion. If you complete a £2,500,000 placing of funds, you will still earn over £37,000 which is not bad for just one project. Just imagine what your bank balance would look like if you only did one or two of those a year. Increase your fees only when you get more experienced and more professional.

Finally, good luck. It was once said that "luck" is when opportunity meets preparedness. Someone else said [I think it was top golfer] that the harder I work, the luckier I get. You have identified a tremendous opportunity. You have everything in this manual to make you as prepared as you could possibly be. Although there is competition, the current decade is the era of the entrepreneur. There are plenty of opportunities to find the right entrepreneurs and plenty of opportunities to find the right investor. Go to the local library and get a few books out on raising Venture Capital and you will see that you now know almost as much as anybody else knows about this business. All you have to do now is go out and do it.

Part 2

Major Organisations

The following are the major organisations with full names and addresses mentioned in Part 1 together with photocopies of relevant papers as appropriate.

1. BVCA stands for The British Venture Capital Association. They can be contacted at Essex House,12/13, Essex Street, London WC2R 3AA. Tel: 071.240.3846. Fax: 071.240.3849. Publications which are available from them free of charge are:

(a) "Business Plans and Financing Proposals", which is written in conjuction with Accountants, Arthur Anderson. This will give you everything you need to write a Business Plan.

(b) A Directory of Members. This will list the major investing organisations who have funds to invest in Venture capital projects.

(c) A Directory of Business Introduction Services. This lists a number of agencies who can introduce your Clients to so called "Business Angels"

(d) "A Guide to Venture Capital". This is another free publication which provides a very useful beginners guide to the Venture Capital and is an excellent companion to this manual.

2. VCR stands for Venture Capital Report. They can be contacted at Freepost 1513, Boston Road, Henley-on-Thames, Oxon. RG9 1BR.
Tel: 0491.579999. Fax: 0491.579825.
Photocopies of various VCR reports are enclosed in Part 3.

3. The Gazette is published by The Capital Exchange, Freepost, Wyvern Centre, Barrs Court Road, Hereford, HR1 1EG.

Tel: 0432.342484. A couple of pages from The Gazette is included in Part 3.

4. Another very useful source of information is from Initiative Europe. They publish a number of newsletters and directories which assist Venture Capital professionals in Europe. They can be contacted at 69, Bondway, London SW8 1SQ. Tel: 071.735.9838. Fax 071.820.0802. A list of their publications is shown n Part 3.

5. Companies House can be contacted at The Registrar of Companies, Crown Way, Maindy, Cardiff CF4 3UZ. Tel 0222.388588. They can give you all the information you need to form a limited company.

6. The Printing Works are a specialist mail order company for business stationery. They can be contacted at 287, Finchley Road, London NW3 6ND. Tel: 071.431.5423. Fax: 071.431.5420.

7. The European Venture Capital Association can be contacted at Minervastraat 6, Box 6, B-1930, Zaventem, Belgium.

Tel +32.2.720.60.10.   Fax: +32.2.725.30.36.

PART 3

Exhibits to assist you in your business

Exhibit 3.1

THE ESTELLE-ALAN CONSULTANCY

HURST HOUSE, CITY ROAD, RADNAGE, BUCKS HP14 4DW.
Mobile 0378.217092 Tel: 0494 483728 Fax: 0494 484039

Business Advisor and Management Consultant to Commerce and Industry for Venture Capital + Commercial Funding

Attn: The Managing Director

If you need Commercial Funding

or Venture Capital Finance

Call us NOW on the above number

We have access to the funds YOU need

The Estelle-Alan Consultancy is a Division of Estelle-Alan International Associates Ltd. V.A.T. No. 606970349
Registered Office: Hurst Cottage, Bottle Square Lane, Radnage, Bucks. HP14 4DP. Registered in England No.1837005

Exhibit 3.2

THE ESTELLE-ALAN CONSULTANCY

HURST HOUSE, CITY ROAD, RADNAGE, BUCKS HP14 4DW.
Mobile:0378 217092 Tel: 0494 483728 Fax: 0494 484039

FACSIMILE TRANSMISSION

PLEASE DELIVER TO ADDRESSEE IMMEDIATELY

ATTENTION: The Managing Director

RE: Commercial Funding/Venture Capital

FROM: Raymond Fox, Managing Director.

TOTAL NO. OF PAGES (including this cover sheet): One

Dear Sir,

My Consultancy has been approached by an Overseas Client who for reasons of confidentiality have asked us not to disclose their identity. My Client wishes to obtain £3M Sterling for an overseas business project. We understand that your organisation have contacts with access to commercial finance/venture capital funds. Can you please drop me a line or send me a fax outlining the services that your organisation provide and the fees you charge. For example, do you charge for preparation of the business proposal, the introduction to the lender, on completion etc? Do you charge on a fee basis or on a % basis? Please outline what information you would require from my Clients to enable you to prepare the appropriate business plan. Some information about your organisation e.g. how long you have been in business, names of references, details of other successful projects etc would also be of interest.

A response by return would be much appreciated. I look forward to hearing from you.

Yours Sincerely,

Raymond Fox

If you do not receive all of the above pages
please contact 0494 483728 or fax 0494 484039

The Estelle-Alan Consultancy is a Division of Estelle-Alan International Associates Ltd. V.A.T. No. 06970349 Registered Office: Hurst Cottage, Bottle Square Lane, Radnage, Bucks. HP14 4DP. Registered in England No.1837005

Exhibit 3.3

BEI ♦ EIB

DEN EUROPÆISKE INVESTERINGSBANK
EUROPAISCHE INVESTITIONSBANK
EYPΩΠΑΙΚΗ ΤΡΑΠΕΖΑ ΕΠΕΝΔΥΣΕΩΝ
EUROPEAN INVESTMENT BANK
BANCO EUROPEO DE INVERSIONES
BANQUE EUROPEENNE D'INVESTISSEMENT
BANCA EUROPEA PER GLI INVESTIMENTI
EUROPESE INVESTERINGSBANK
BANCO EUROPEU DE INVESTIMENTO
EUROOPAN INVESTOINTIPANKKI
EUROPEISKA INVESTERINGSBANKEN

EIB FINANCE IN THE UNITED KINGDOM

Introduction

The European Investment Bank (EIB) was set up in 1958 under the Treaty of Rome to provide loan finance for capital investment furthering European Union policy objectives. It supports viable projects in the following categories:

- regional development;
- transport and telecommunications;
- energy;
- environmental protection;
- competitiveness and integration of industry, and
- small and medium sized enterprises.

The EIB also provides, within set limits, finance outside the European Union in the framework of the Union's co-operation policy with non-member countries. Owned by the EU Member States, the EIB raises its funds on capital markets where its bond issues have consistently received an excellent credit rating (AAA).

The EIB's approach

The EIB is a source of flexible medium and long-term funds. It provides loan finance in two main ways:

1. **direct loans** (or finance for "big-ticket" leasing) for capital spending programmes or projects costing more than about £20 million (ECU 25 million). Borrowers/lessees with such programmes, and larger companies should contact the EIB directly, or in conjunction with their bankers, to examine how they might qualify for EIB support and to discuss their financing needs.

2. **loan facilities to banks and financial institutions** (including leasing companies) to help them provide finance to customers with eligible spending programmes or projects that may individually be up to about £20 million. Lending decisions under these schemes remain with the clearing bank or finance house with access to EIB funds.

100, Boulevard Konrad Adenauer - L-2950 Luxembourg - Tél. (+352) 43 79 1 - Tx. (+) 3530 bnkeu lu - Fax (+352) 43 77 04
H320 Vidéoconférence (+352) 43 93 67

28

Exhibit 3.4

2

<u>EIB loan schemes via banks/finance houses: qualification criteria</u>

A small or medium sized enterprise (SME) with a fixed asset investment of at least £33,000 (ECU 40,000), may be considered for EIB funding regardless of where it is located. The investment may be in industry, the hotel/tourism sector, leisure, wholesale or retail trade or in providing services (including those for private consumers); but housing, health, social work and schools do not qualify. Short term finance for property developers is also excluded.

To qualify as an SME, a company must have:
- fewer than 500 employees (exceptions possible for labour intensive businesses), and
- not more than about £60 million (ECU 75 million) net fixed assets per the balance sheet (i.e. gross fixed assets less accumulated depreciation).

A project (or programme) of up to £20 million promoted by a company or entity that is <u>not an SME</u>, may be considered as eligible within these EIB loan schemes via the banks if it is for energy saving, environmental protection, is aimed at improving industrial competitiveness or is a qualifying infrastructure investment. Even if it is not eligible under these categories (energy, environment etc.), it may still be dealt with within these loan facilities, on an exceptional basis provided it benefits regional development. Large companies should in any event consider contacting EIB directly.

EIB funding for an individual project can be up to 50% of the gross project cost (comprising capital costs and directly related working capital requirements).

A project that includes the acquisition of <u>second-hand</u> fixed assets (property or machinery) will be eligible only if:
(a)   the EIB has not already funded the fixed assets in question; and
(b)   the second-hand assets represent not more than half of the project cost;
        this requirement, however, does not apply if the project cost is less than £295,000* (ECU 350,000).

The purchase of land can be financed only if it represents a small part of the total project cost.

There are no job creation criteria, but the EIB is interested in the estimated number of jobs likely to be created or maintained by each project.

---

*   At November 1995 conversion rate of 1 ECU = £0.84

29

Exhibit 3.5

3

<u>Points of Contact</u>

For projects up to about £20 million (ECU 25 million) please contact any of the following banks or finance houses that have access to EIB funding facilities:

Barclays Bank PLC
Mr Martin Moran, or
Mr Adrian Black
European Loans Unit
P.O. Box 256
Fleetway House
1st Floor
25 Farringdon Street
London EC4A 4LP
Tel   0171-832 3084 or 3085 (direct lines)
Fax 0171-832 3086

**Barclays Mercantile Business Finance
Limited**
Mr Garry Clarke
Pricing Manager
Miss Wendy Horstman, or
Miss Karen Newsome
Finance Department
Churchill Plaza
Churchill Way
Basingstoke
Hampshire RG21 1GL
Tel   01256-791690 (direct line Mr Clarke)
        01256-791867 (direct line Miss Horstman)
        01256-791173 (direct line Miss Newsome)
Fax 01256-791664

Midland Bank plc
Mr Richard Watson
Loan Schemes Unit, Branch Banking
Griffin House
41 Silver Street Head
Sheffield S1 1RG
Tel   0114-252 9316
Fax 0114-252 9770

Forward Trust Business Finance Limited
Mr Mike Barnes
Product Manager
P.O. Box 1811
Metropolitan House
1 Hagley Road
Edgbaston
Birmingham B16 8SS
Tel   0121-455 4584 (direct)
Fax 0121-455 4620

Yorkshire Bank PLC
Mr David W. Roxby
Senior Marketing Manager
Business Services
Brunswick Point
Wade Lane
Leeds LS2 8NQ
Tel   0113-231 5325 (direct)
Fax 0113-231 5166

Bank of Wales PLC
Mr Charles Bithell, Manager
Risk Management Department
Kingsway
Cardiff CF1 4YB
Tel   01222-787443 (direct)
        01222-229922 (switchboard)
Fax 01222-397193

Exhibit 3.6

4

The Royal Bank of Scotland plc
Mr Mike Rabone
Assistant Manager, Loan Schemes
Branch Banking Division
Commercial Banking Services
P.O. Box 31
42 St Andrew Square
Edinburgh EH2 2YE
Tel   0131-523 2091 (direct)
      0131-556 8555 (switchboard)
Fax 0131-558 3765

RoyScot Trust plc
Mr David Gray, Marketing Manager, or
Mr Geoffrey Slade, Business Sales Manager
RoyScot House
The Promenade
Cheltenham
Gloucestershire GL50 1PL
Tel 01242-224455 (switchboard)
Fax 01242-570524

Bank of Scotland
Ms Maureen McCole, Assistant Manager
Business Banking
UK Banking - East
P.O. Box No. 12
Uberior House
61 Grassmarket
Edinburgh EH1 2JF
Tel   0131-243 5944 (direct)
      0131-442 7777 (switchboard)
Fax 0131-243 5738

NWS BANK plc
Mr Michael R. Perry
General Manager
NWS House
City Road
Chester X CH99 3AN
Tel   01244-693463 (direct)
      01244-690000 (switchboard)
Fax 01244-693006

Clydesdale Bank PLC
Mr James Watson
Development Manager Business Markets
30 St Vincent Place
Glasgow G1 2HL
Tel   0141-223 2229 (direct)
Fax 0141-223 2221

Clyde General Finance Limited
Mr David W. Bell
Credit & Leasing Manager
Mirren Court One
119 Renfrew Road
Paisley PA3 4EA
Tel   0141-848 6844 (direct)
Tel   0141-887 3070 (switchboard)
Fax 0141-840 1807

Northern Bank Limited
Mr Michael Reid
Marketing Executive (Business
Marketing & Customer Service)
P.O. Box 183
2nd Floor, 14 Donegal Square West
Belfast BT1 6JS
Tel   01232-245277 (switchboard)
Fax 01232-330169

Northern Bank Leasing Group
Mr Bev Douglas
Manager
PO Box 173
Northern Court
16-18 Gloucester Street
Belfast BT1 4AH
Tel 01232-438557 (switchboard)
Fax 01232-320010

Ulster Bank Limited
Mr Michael Rogan
Senior Advances Manager
Avenue House
42/44 Rosemary Street
Belfast BT1 1QE
Tel 01232-898101
Fax 01232-898210

Lombard & Ulster Limited
Mr Allan Palmer
Manager, Planning and Marketing
40 Linenhall Street
Belfast BT2 8DF
Tel   01232-897580 (direct)
      01232-329261 (switchboard)
Fax 01232-897571

31

Exhibit 3.7

5

Ulster Bank - Corporate Banking
Mr Mark Johnston
Senior Manager
Bulloch House
2 Linenhall Street
Belfast BT2 8BA
Tel 01232-326222 (switchboard)
Fax 01232-241460

First Trust Bank
Mr Dennis Licence
Head of Corporate and Commercial Banking
4 Queens Square
Belfast BT1 3DJ
Tel 01232-325599 (switchboard)
Fax 01232-231010

First Trust Finance & Leasing
Mr Tony Finlay
Sales and Development Manager
First Trust Centre
92 Ann Street
Belfast BT1 3HH
Tel 01232-325599 / 242423 (switchboard)
     Ext. 40181
Fax 01232-247131

Bank of Ireland
Mr Frank Boyle
Business Manager Northern Ireland
Retail Sales and Marketing Division
54 Donegall Place
Belfast BT1 5BX
Tel 01232-246752 (direct)
     01232-234334 (switchboard)
Fax 01232-329182

NIIB Group Limited
Mr Lawrence Kinney
Administration Controller
32 Central Avenue
Bangor
CO Down BT20 3AS
Tel 01247-469415 (switchboard)
Fax 01247-461434

Other banks may be added to this list.

For projects of more than £20 million:

European Investment Bank
London Office
68 Pall Mall
London SW1Y 5ES
Tel: 0171-343 1200
Fax: 0171-930 9929

GMB November 1995

Exhibit 3.8

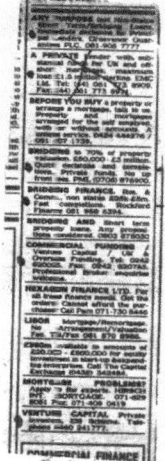

Exhibit 3.9

STANDARD CONFIDENTIALITY LETTER

[on notepaper of supplier of confidential information, e.g vendor or his agent]

To: [Potential Investor]

Dear Sirs

We understand that you wish to investigate the business of [*name of company*] (the "Company") [and of its subsidiaries] (together the "Group") [in connection with [*insert nature of transaction*] (the "Permitted Purpose")] and that you, your directors and employees, other potential syndicate members or other providers of finance and your financial and professional advisers in relation to the Permitted Purpose, (together referred to as the "Disclosees"), will need access to certain information relating to the Group (the "Confidential Information") [including, without limitation: ....].

1.   In consideration of our agreeing to supply, and so supplying, the Confidential Information to you and agreeing to enter into discussions with you, you hereby undertake and agree as follows:-

(a)   to hold the Confidential Information in confidence and not to disclose or
to   permit it to be made available to any person, firm or company (except other Disclosees), without our prior [written] consent;

(b)   only to use the Confidential Information for the Permitted Purpose [provided that on being notified by us that the proposals concerning the Permitted Purpose have lapsed, you may approach the Company [or its advisers] with separate proposals and we acknowledge that in so doing you may have regard to the Confidential Information provided];

(c)   to ensure that each person to whom disclosure of Confidential Information is made by you is fully aware in advance of your obligation under this letter and that, in the case of other potential syndicate members, each such person gives an undertaking in respect of the Confidential Information, in the terms of this letter;

Exhibit 3.10

(d) upon written demand from us either to return the Confidential Information and any copies of it or to confirm to us in writing that, save as required by law or regulation, it has been destroyed. You shall not be required to return reports, notes or other material prepared by you or other Disclosees or on your or their behalf which incorporate Confidential Information ("Secondary Information") provided that the Secondary Information is kept confidential;

(e) to keep confidential and not reveal to any person, firm or company (other than Disclosees) the fact of your investigations into the Group or that discussions or negotiations are taking place or have taken place between us in connection with the proposed transaction or that potential investors/acquirers are being sought for the Company:

(f) that no person gives any warranty or makes any representation as to the accuracy or otherwise of the Confidential Information, save as may subsequently be agreed.

2. Nothing in paragraph 1(a) to (f) of this letter shall apply to any information or Confidential Information:

(a) which at the time of its disclosure is in the public domain;

(b) which after disclosure comes into the public domain for any reason except your failure, or failure on the part of any Disclosee, to comply with the terms of this letter;

(c) which is disclosed by us or the Company, its directors, employees or advisers on a non-confidential basis;

(d) which was lawfully in your possession prior to such disclosure;

(e) which is subsequently received by you from a third party without obligations of confidentiality (and, for the avoidance of doubt, you shall not be required to enquire whether there is a duty of confidentiality); or

(f) which you or a Disclosee are required to disclose, retain or maintain by law or any regulatory or government authority.

Exhibit 3.11

3. In consideration of the undertakings given by you in this letter, we undertake and agree:

    (a) to disclose Confidential Information to you;

    (b) to keep confidential and not to reveal to any person, firm or company (other than persons within our group who need to know, our bankers and professional advisers) the fact of your investigation into the Group or that discussions or negotiations are taking place or have taken place between us; (and

    (c) that we will not prior to [*insert date*], directly or indirectly enter into negotiations or have discussions of any kind with any other potential investors which relate to the Permitted Purpose without your prior written consent and we recognise that in reliance on this undertaking you and other Disclosees may incur substantial costs.) (This relates to exclusivity and is a matter for negotiation).

4. (a) This letter shall be governed by and construed in accordance with English law [and the parties irrevocably submit to the non-exclusive jurisdiction of the Courts of England and Wales in respect of any claim, dispute or difference arising out of or in connection with this letter.]

    (b) The obligations in this letter will terminate on [*insert expiry date*].

Please indicate your acceptance of the above by signing and returning the enclosed copy of this letter as soon as possible.

Yours faithfully

On copy;

We have read and agree to the terms of the above letter.

Signed by   )
for and on behalf of   )
)
LIMITED   )

Date: [.....................]

Exhibit 3.12

VCR — Venture Capital Report
– The link between investors and entrepreneurs –

Contents
August 1994

Successful Match **Inshore Marine Salvage — £100,000**

A VCR subscriber has invested £100,000 in an inshore marine salvage project, headed by Steve Cox and Nicholas Pearson. They had collected a database of wrecks, mainly in Lyme Bay, Dorset, from which cargoes such as steel, coal and marble could be readily recovered and landed at Torquay for sale to salvage dealers. The investment was for £20,000 more than the principals originally sought, and was made for 33% of the equity, rather than 25% as outlined in the original VCR article in January 1994. In April 1994 a suitable vessel was purchased and now that remedial work has been completed or the vessel, diving has started on a wreck 40 miles off Great Yarmouth, Norfolk.   Page 6

1. Malt Whisky Distillery — £400,000   **Scotland**

A family team of father and two sons are creating a new malt whisky distillery on the Isle of Arran. The father has spent his entire career in the whisky industry. The principals have already generated £633,000 from 1,500 purchasers of whisky 'bonds' of five cases of blended and five cases of single malt whisky to be delivered in 2001. These funds will be used to finance working capital, and can be drawn down from the trust in which they are held, as whisky is produced, bottled and put into bond. The family is investing £200,000, and additional equity of £400,000 is sought towards the total funding required of £1m. The balance will be through grant and loan. Annual pre-tax profits are forecast to increase from £290,000 in year 1 to £452,000 in 2001, when the first single malt bottles will be delivered. 66% of the equity is offered.   Page 7

2. Postcard Advertising — £260,000   **London/International**

Two young Swedish entrepreneurs started a business in 1991 selling advertising via postcards placed in racks in the leading fashionable restaurants in Stockholm. The objective was to sell to advertisers the ability to reach opinion leaders and trend setters, who are extremely difficult to reach through normal media channels. The artistic content of the postcards must be of the highest quality, so that the rack of cards is always of interest to restaurant clientele. One of the founders moved to London in 1992 to start the UK business. It is now making profits of £10,000 per month on average. The two entrepreneurs now seek finance to start up in New York, Los Angeles and San Francisco. As the idea is not protectable they believe they must move quickly to capture the market. £260,000 is sought, and 35% of the equity is offered. Profits of $1m are projected by year 4.   Page 11

3. Furniture, Arts & Crafts Retailer — £150,000   **London**

A company well known in its niche market, had been sourcing, importing, wholesaling and retailing high quality furniture, arts and crafts in the UK, when it went into receivership in 1992, due to the recession and overstocking, with a turnover of £2.9m. An entrepreneur purchased the business from the receiver and sold on the wholesaling arm. The new company now has six retail outlets and has completed 18 months' trading. Turnover for the first year was £1m and profits were £15,000 before tax. Current year turnover is on target for £1.5m, and a profit of £23,000 is forecast, rising to sales of £2.8m with a profit of £335,000 in 1996. The entrepreneur now seeks an additional £150,000 in order to finance more rapid expansion by opening two new shops and setting up a franchise structure. 21% of the equity is offered.   Page 16

4. Medical Diagnostics MBO — £1.2m   **International**

A Swiss based company which manufactures medical diagnostic kits has developed a new breath test for the bacteria Helicobacter pylori, which has been associated with peptic ulcers and gastro-intestinal complaints. The company recently completed a buy-out from its parent and the managing director seeks an additional £1.2m to complete the funding package. He is projecting pre-tax profits of £2,222,000 in year 3. 40% of the equity is available.   Page 21

5. Australia Travel Guides — £113,000   **International**

Two entrepreneurs intend to form a new business to publish detailed local area travel guides for use by UK tourists to Australia, capitalising on the increasing number of UK tourists prior to the 2000 Sydney Olympic games. Revenue will be generated by selling 40 pages of advertising in each 64 page guide. Each guide will cover a specific area, such as Sydney, Brisbane, Hunter Valley, the Great Barrier Reef etc. The concept was tested with one guide to date; the UK backer at the time did not provide sufficient funds to allow the project to start on a big enough scale. £113,000 is sought to set up the business, including the publication of 7 regional guides in year 1. In year 2, a further 16 guides will be published. Pre-tax profits of £356,000 are forecast on revenue of £1.39m in year 2, and the equity is offered.   Page 26

Copyright © August 1994, Venture Capital Report Ltd, Boston Road, Henley-on-Thames, Oxon. RG9 1DY, UK. Tel: 01491 ...

Exhibit 3.13

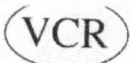

(VCR) Venture Capital Report
— The link between investors and entrepreneurs —

Contents
September 1994

Successful Match   **Hungarian Wine Importer — £25,000**

A VCR subscriber has invested a first tranche of £25,000 in Marybelle (UK) Ltd, an Hungarian wine importing business run by Andrew Breiger and David Miller, which featured in the August 1994 issue of VCR. The wine is imported from the Bonanal winery, 5km outside of Kiskoros in southern Hungary, and capital was sought to provide sufficient marketing support. A retired accountant himself, the investor will join the company as part time finance director. The investment is for a 33% equity stake with the balance provided as a loan.

Page 6

1. Down's Syndrome Diagnosis — £100,000+   **South East**

A small UK biotechnology company, founded in 1991, is achieving sales of its first product: fluorescent labelled DNA probes for the detection of genetic defects. It has signed a worldwide marketing agreement with a US company. Its latest kit will detect Down's Syndrome from a sample of 10ml of mother's blood at eight weeks, the test taking only a few hours to perform, at a suggested price of £15 per test. Current genetic tests cost £150, involve some risk to the mother and foetus, take three weeks, and can only be done at 16 weeks. There are other biochemical tests but these give only a probability and are not definitive. The company has 2.2m shares in issue and has been raising capital by issuing shares at £2 per share. It has recently been offered £100,000 for 50,000 shares. It seeks to raise up to £500,000 by the issue of shares at £2 per share. It hopes to achieve a listing on a stock market in 1996 or 1997.

Page 7

2. Pub Entertainment Systems — £100,000   **South East**

A business was set up in 1993 to develop a control system to deliver a range of pub entertainment including primarily audio and video jukeboxes, satellite and terrestrial television and background music. Hitherto each of these have been delivered and controlled separately in the pub which has meant that rather than being used to maximum effect, they have competed with each other to the detriment of the pub's atmosphere and therefore its turnover. The new system allows the landlord to programme each form of entertainment to play when required during the day and a zoning facility allows him to play each simultaneously if required in different parts of the pub. The system has been developed over the last two years and is believed to be unique. It has been trialled by some brewers over the last year, and the first months' sales targets have been met. Pre tax profits are forecast to rise from £70,000 in year 1 to £120,000 in year 3 with revenues from new related products not yet included in these projections. £100,000 is sought for 39% of the equity. Page 14

3. Hole-in-One Insurance — up to £100,000   **International**

Hole-in-one insurance is big business in the US. Companies, often car dealers, pay a premium of perhaps $400, enabling them to sponsor a competition or charity event, putting up a $20,000 car as a prize. If a competitor scores a hole-in-one then the insurance company pays the dealer. One US company now has hole-in-one premium income of over $15m pa. The market for sponsored hole-in-one events has grown with the availability of the insurance. The president and founder of the recently established third largest hole-in-one insurance company in the US now plans to set up a similar business in the UK. He seeks up to £100,000 to establish a pilot operation to test the UK market and seeks an investor who can offer help and support in the UK. He envisages a 50/50 joint venture, after the investor recovers his initial investment.

Page 19

4. Improved Glider — £125,000   **South East**

The creator of the revolutionary Optica aeroplane has spent the last six years, supported by a series of government grants, developing an improved method of fabricating light aircraft, using rigid honeycomb structure panels which are cut very accurately using computer controlled machinery and then bonded. The first prototype aircraft to demonstrate this method of construction is a glider and will have its first flight in October or November 1994. £120,000 is sought to build the first production prototype, to obtain certification and to obtain the first sales of the glider. It is hoped that the technology may subsequently be applied to the manufacture of several types of aircraft and also licensed to other manufacturers abroad. 25% of the equity is offered.

Page 22

A four page write-up on each venture, with full financial and contact details, prepared by VCR after meeting the entrepreneur, is published in the monthly report. Given for free from subscription.

Copyright © September 1994, Venture Capital Report Ltd, Boston Road, Henley on Thames, RG9 1DY, UK. Tel (0491) Stport Fax (0491) 571188

Exhibit 3.14

6th edition of VCR Guide to Venture Capital in the UK & Europe

Special Offer
£50 off
Discount Price
UK £56, Europe £60, USA £70

- 1,184 page guide on how and where to raise capital from over 1,000 sources of venture capital, including biographies of executives and investment portfolios of the major venture capital companies.

- Portfolios provide details of the actual investments made in companies (successes and failures): name, location and nature of business; date, type, amount of investment, % equity and other financial data; and description of progress since investment.

- New section on 'Business Angels' gives contact details of schemes of private investors looking to back small businesses.

- Providers of venture capital use it to keep abreast of competitors' actual performance, and to identify appropriate partners for joint ventures and syndicated deals.

- Seekers of venture capital, and their advisors, use to to target investors and to identify which particular executive to approach, as opposed to an untargeted 'Dear Sir' letter.

- Used by: Venture capital companies; Banks; Entrepreneurs & inventors; Corporate finance firms; Financial advisors & brokers; Finance directors; Accountants & Solicitors; & Libraries.

Reviews of the Guide

"the most comprehensive coverage of the industry ... a number of accountants produce free lists of venture capital organisations while the BVCA and EVCA both have directories of members. None, however, has the detail which the would-be entrepreneur or inventor will find in this guide." **Financial Times**

"a superb book that must be a venture capitalist's dream. It 's also essential for any entrepreneurs seeking money. With this book in your hand you are an instant expert. Recommended." **Business Age**

"the source book for providers and seekers of cash, for brokers and banks and, indeed, for the whole sector ... enables the reader to separate claims from the facts in a hype-prone business." **Daily Telegraph**

"We find the company profiles the best one-stop source of competitor information. We use the profiles constantly to track competitor performance and portfolio strategy." **Apax Partners & Co**

"A key insight into any venture capital firm is provided by a detailed tabulation regarding the ventures it has backed ... yours is the only book in the world that contains such tabulations. The thanks I've received for recommending your book are legion."
Baring Venture Partners

Exhibit 3.15

Business Money - Special Feature

Banks Lenders Addresses

KEY: ● = Contact a local branch if it is listed in your telephone directory ; ○ = Smaller Society ; 1 = May have fixed rate money available ; 2 = May require borrower's current account 3 = Will lend under DTI Small Firms Loan Guarantee Scheme ; 4 = Will allow repayment by endowment/pension policy ; 5 = Will give APR quotes

BANKS	ADDRESSES	1	2	3	4	5	COMMENTS
ABBEY NATIONAL	Abbey House, 201 Grafton Gate East, Milton Keynes MK9 1AN T 0908 344962 F 0908 344403				●		May do semi-commercial.
AIB BANK	● Bankcentre-Britain, Belmont Road, Uxbridge, Middlesex. UB8 1SA T 0895 272222 F 0895 239734	●	●	●	●		Will consider any good proposal. Strong on healthcare.
AITKEN HUME BANK PLC	30 City Road, London EC1Y 2AY T 071 638 5070 F 071 588 9837	●	●			●	Providing working capital finance to business.
ALLIED TRUST BANK	Granite Hse, 97-101 Cannon St, London EC4 5AD T 071 283 9111 F 071 626 1213				●	●	Bank charges winner. 10-year property lender.
ANGLO IRISH BANKCORP	Moor House, 119 London Wall, London EC2Y 5ET T 071 628 4004 F 071 628 4450	●					Property lender to 15 years.
BANK OF IRELAND	34 High Street, Slough, Berkshire, SL1 1ED T 0733 517777 F 0735 517222	●	●	●	●	●	Selective property lender. Strong on healthcare.
BANK JULIUS BAER & CO LTD	Bevis Marks Hse, Bevis Marks, London EC3M 7NE T 071 623 4211 F 071 283 6146	●					Lender to investment property.
BANK OF SCOTLAND	● Head Office, The Mount, Edinburgh EH1 1YZ T 031 346 6233 F 031 346 6089	●	●	●	●		Selective major bank.
BANK OF WALES	● Head Office, Kingsway, Cardiff CF1 4YB T 0222 229922 F 0222 397193	●	●		●		Curr a/c's & loans for £1m t/o £200k Net with £50k Net prof Cos and above.
BARCLAYS BANK PLC	● PO Box 120, Longwood Close, Westwood Business Pk, Coventry CV4 8JN T 0203 532447 F 0203 532497/8	●	●	●	●	●	Will consider any good proposal.
BELMONT BANK	37-43 Sackville Street, London W1X 1DB T 071 413 5000 F 071 734 6071					●	Flexible smaller bank, will consider any sound proposal up to £150k.
BNP MORTGAGES	● 8-13 King William St, London EC4N 7BL T 071 929 2274 F 071 895 7449						Not actively lending at present.
CALEDONIAN BANK PLC	8 St Andrew Square, Edinburgh EH22 2PP T 031 556 6235 F 031 556 5338						Edinburgh based commercial property lender.
CHARTERHOUSE BANK LTD	1 Paternoster Row, St Paul's, London EC4M 7DH T 071 248 4000 F 071 248 4317	●					Investment property and development funder.
CITIBANK TRUST LTD	St Martins House, 1 Hammersmith Grove, London W6 0NY T 081 741 8000 F 081 741 5863						Energetic commercial mortgage lender.
CLOSE BROTHERS LTD	36 Great St Helens St, London EC3A 6AP T 071 283 2241 F 071 623 9699						A smashing bank. Will look at anything sensible including development.
CLYDESDALE BANK PLC	● PO Box 43, 30 St Vincent Place, Glasgow G1 2HL T 041 248 7070 F 041 204 0828	●	●	●	●	●	Another bank which has its act together. Any good proposition welcome.
CONFEDERATION BANK LTD	Bank House, Primett Road, Stevenage, Herts. SG1 3UQ T 0438 744550 F 0438 744556	●	●			●	Will look at good semi-commercial in many sectors.
CO-OPERATIVE BANK	● PO Box 101, 1 Balloon Street, Manchester M60 4EP T 061 832 3456 F 061 829 4475	●	●	●	●	●	Has its ethical code. Will look at most things which fit it.
CREDIT LYONNAIS	84-94 Queen Victoria Street, London EC4P 4LX T 071 634 8000 F 071 489 1559	●	●				Is determined to build a UK presence organically. Selective approach.
DUNBAR BANK PLC	9 Sackville Street, Piccadilly, London W1A 2JP T 071 437 7844 F 071 437 3953						Investment, commercial property and development lender.
EXETER BANK	Exeter Trust House, Blackboy Road, Exeter EX4 6SE T 0392 50635 F 0392 77798				●		Respected business property lender.
FIRST TRUST BANK	4 Queens Square, Belfast BT1 3DJ T 0232 325599						New entry in our tables. Full details next month.
GIROBANK PLC	● Newton House, 101-113 Pentonville Road, London N1 9XB T 071 833 8111 F 071 833 8194		●				Not actively lending. Will help sub-post offices. Top cash handler.
GRANVILLE TRUST LTD	Mint House, 77 Mansell Street, London E1 8AF T 071 488 1212 F 071 709 0346						Friendly, smaller property lender. Retail & development strengths.
HAMBURGISCHE LANDESBANK	Moorgate Hall, 155 Moorgate, London EC2M 6XB T 071 972 9292						Range of loan and overdraft services to business in the £3m + sector.
HAMPSHIRE TRUST PLC	28E West Street, Fareham, Hants. PO16 0AJ T 0329 234294 F 0329 285910	●			●		Will consider any good property deal. Rapid initial response.
HERITABLE AND GENERAL INVESTMENT BANK LTD	52 Berkeley Square, London W1X 6EH T 071 493 6621 F 071 529 1958						Discreet London based bank.
HYPOBANK	● 41 Moorgate, London EC2R 9AB T 071 638 2728 F 071 638 1709	●					German owned, likes chunky blue chip investments deals. Manchester and London.
JULIAN HODGE BANK	10 Windsor Place, Cardiff CF1 3BX T 0222 220800 F 0222 344061	●				●	Care, professionals & light industry.

Exhibit 3.16

Business Money · Special Feature

BANKS	ADDRESSES	1	2	3	4	5	COMMENTS
KREDIETFINANCE CORPORATION LIMITED	14-15 Quarry Street, Guildford, Surrey. GU1 3UY T 0483 504290						Commercial mortgage lender. Will appear in the tables next month.
LEOPOLD JOSEPH & SONS	29 Gresham Street, London EC2V 7EA T 071 588 2323 F 071 725 0105	•	•			•	London based selective property funder.
LLOYDS BANK PLC ●	PO Box 112, Canons Way, Bristol BS99 7LB T 0272 433433 F 0272 423006	•	•	•	•	•	Just launched small business campaign.
W M MANN & CO (INVESTMENTS) LTD	201 Bath Street, Glasgow G2 4HY T 041 248 4936 F 041 229 2976	•				•	Versatile Glasgow based supporter of Scottish property.
MEES PIERSON	Princes House, 95 Gresham Street, London EC2V 7NA T 071 606 4022 F 071 603 0827	•					Working capital funder in £10m+ turnover business.
MIDLAND BANK PLC ●	Griffin House, 41 Silver Street Head, Sheffield S1 3GG T 0742 529445 F 0742 529312	•	•	•	•	•	Now doing some good deals and regaining business market share.
NATIONAL WESTMINSTER BANK LIMITED ●	Level 10, Drapers Gardens, 12 Throgmorton Avenue, London EC2N 2DL T 071 920 5555 F 071 458 2111	•	•	•	•	•	Loves doing business, a bruiser. Will look at anything good.
NORTHERN BANK	PO Box 183, Donegall Square West, Belfast BT1 5JS T 0232 245277 F 0232 251349	•	•	•	•	•	Will look at any good proposal in Northern Ireland.
ROBERT FLEMING & CO	Boking Admin Cntr, Sovereign Hse, 16-22 Western Rd, Romford RM1 3LB T 0708 766966 F 071 377 2235	•	•				Selective lenders, mainly investment property at present.
ROYAL BANK OF SCOTLAND ●	42 Islington High Street, London N1 8XI. T 071 833 2121	•	•	•	•	•	Another 1-11 banc. Will look at anything sound from the UK.
SINGER & FRIEDLANDER LIMITED	21 New Street, Bishopsgate, London EC2M 4HR T 071 623 3000 F 071 628 2122	•					An active player in the commercial field. Wears a merchant bank hat sometimes.
SVENSKA INTERNATIONAL	Svenska House, 3-5 Newgate Street, London EC1A 7DA T 071 329 4487 F 071 329 0036/37	•					Larger figure lender to investment/industrial property.
TSB BANK PLC ●	Victoria House, Victoria Square, Birmingham B1 1EZ T 021 600 6000 F 021 600 5114/5	•	•	•	•	•	Back into profit. Looking for business.
TYNDALL BANK PLC	29-35 Princess Victoria Street, Clifton, Bristol BS8 4BY T 0273 744720 F 0272 741745						Does not lend. Offers business bank account for those who always operate in credit.
UCB	UCB House, 36-60 Sutton Court Road, Sutton, Surrey SM1 4TE T 081 401 4000 F 081 401 4888	•					Active throughout the recession. Just looking at investment & cann sector now.
ULC TRUST LIMITED ●	1 Great Cumberland Place, London W1H 7AL T 071 258 0094 F 071 268 4273						Up to £150k development and bridging loan specialist.
ULSTER BANK LIMITED	PO Box 232, 47 Donegall Place, Belfast BT1 5AL T 0232 244744	•	•	•	•	•	Will look at anything sound in Northern Ireland.
UNITED BANK OF KUWAIT	3 Lombard Street, London EC3V 9DT T 071 487 6500 F 071 481 6947	•				•	Likes investment property and good classity pre-let commercial development deals.
WESTERN TRUST & SAVINGS	The Moneycentre, Plymouth PL1 1SE T 0752 224141 F 0752 269236	•				•	Plymouth based investment property & commercial development funder.
YORKSHIRE BANK ●	20 Merrion Way, Leeds LS2 8NZ T 0532 315000 F 0532 420733	•	•	•	•	•	A great 1-11 banc will look at anything sound.
BUILDING SOCIETIES							
BARNSLEY ○	Permanent Building, Regent Street, Barnsley, South Yorkshire S70 2EH T 0226 733099 F 0226 287334				•		Is doing very little commercial. Must be in South Yorkshire.
BEVERLEY ○	57 Market Place, Beverley, Humberside HU17 8AA T 0482 881510 F 0482 872680				•		Will look at some proposals close to Beverley.
BIRMINGHAM MIDSHIRES	PO Box 81, 35-49 Lichfield Street, Wolverhampton WV1 1EL T 0902 710710 F 0902 322510	•			•		Active. Commercial mortgage lender.
BRADFORD & BINGLEY	Bingley Operations Centre, PO Box 2, Bingley, West Yorkshire BD16 2LW T 0274 555555 F 0274 569116	•					Investment property, professionals, shops, offices industrial.
BRISTOL & WEST	PO Box 27, Broad Quay, Bristol BS99 7AX T 0272 294271 F 0272 452724	•					Good investment property. Occasional factory, shop or office.
CAMBRIDGE	32 St Andrews Street, Cambridge CB2 3AR T 0223 315440 F 0223 302502				•		Active commercially, 30 miles of Cambridge.
CHELSEA	Thirlestaine Road, Cheltenham, Glos. GL53 7AL T 0242 521391 F 0242 578411				•		Not actively promoting.
CHELTENHAM & GLOUCESTER	Barnett Way, Gloucester GL4 7RL T 0452 372372 F 0452 323171				•		Not actively lending at present.
DERBYSHIRE	Duffield Hall, Duffield, Derby DE5 1AG T 0332 841791 F 0332 841791				•		Selectively lending. Derby postcode area.
DUNFERMLINE	PO Box 4, East Port, Dunfermline, Fife KY12 7LO T 0383 721621 F 0383 622580				•		Strong involvement with good proposals in Scotland & Manchester.

Exhibit 3.17

Business Money - Special Feature

BUILDING SOCIETIES	ADDRESSES	1	2	3	4	5	COMMENTS
ECOLOGY	18 Station Road, Cross Hills, Nr Keighley, West Yorkshire BD20 7EH T 0535 635933 F 0535 636166				*		Semi-commercial with environmentally acceptable theme.
HALIFAX	Trinity Road, Halifax, West Yorks. HX1 2RG T 0422 333333 F 0422 333010/332041				*		Not actively promoting.
HINCKLEY & RUGBY	Upper Bond Street, Hinckley, Leics. LE10 1DG T 0455 251234 F 0455 618506	*			*		Active in most property sectors with sound proposals.
HOLMESDALE	43 Church Street, Reigate, Surrey RH2 0AE T 0737 245716 F 0737 246962				*		Occasional commercial close to Reigate.
KENT RELIANCE	Reliance House, Manor Road, Chatham, Kent ME4 6AF T 0634 848944 F 0634 830942				*		Will consider good proposals in Kent.
MANCHESTER	18-20 Bridge Street, Manchester M3 3BU T 061 834 9465 F 061 833 2796				*		Semi-commercial in the Manchester area.
MELTON MOWBRAY	39 Nottingham St, Melton Mowbray, Leics. LE13 1NR T 0664 63937 F 0664 480205				*		Will consider commercial close to home.
NATIONAL & PROVINCIAL	Provincial House, Bradford, West Yorkshire BD1 1NL T 0274 733444 F 0274 84585				*		Not actively promoting.
NATIONAL COUNTIES	147 High Street, Epsom, Surrey KT19 8EN T 0372 742211 F 0372 745607				*		Lends to a wide range of property transactions.
NATIONWIDE	Croft Campus, Pipers Way, Swindon, Wiltshire SN3 1TA T 0793 510703 F 0793 510431				*		Actively lending a range of commercial mortgages.
NEWBURY	17-20 Bartholomew Street, Newbury, Berkshire RG1 5LY T 0635 43676 F 0635 38790				*		Will look at most good property proposals.
NORTHERN ROCK	Northern Rock House, Gosforth, Newcastle-Upon-Tyne NE3 4PL T 091 285 7191 F 091 2130820	*			*		Active on a wide range of commercial mortgages.
NORWICH & PETERBOROUGH	Peterborough Business Park, Lynch Wood, Peterborough PE2 6WZ T 0733 371371 F 0733 371372	*			*		Active on a wide range of commercial mortgages.
PENRITH	7 King Street, Penrith, Cumbria CA11 7AR T 0768 63675				*		May consider close to home.
PORTMAN	25 High Street, Marlborough, Wilts. SN8 1NF T 0672 514371 F 0672 517300	*			*		Good investment property and professionals.
SAFFRON WALDEN HERTS & ESSEX	Market Place, Saffron Walden, Essex CB10 1HX T 0799 522211 F 0799 513622				*		The occasional agricultural or professional, must have residence.
WEST BROMWICH	374 High Street, West Bromwich, West Midlands B70 8LR T 021 525 7070 F 021 500 5961				*		Active commercial mortgage lender.
WEST CUMBRIA	Cumbria House, Murray Road, Workington, Cumbria CA14 2AD T 0900 605717 F 0900 68767				*		May consider close to home.
WOOLWICH	Watling Street, Bexley Heath, Kent DA6 7RR T 081 298 5000				*		May consider semi-commercial.
FINANCE HOUSES							
AGRICULTURAL MORTGAGE CORP. PLC	AMC House, Chantry Street, Andover, Hampshire SP10 1DD T 0262 334334 F 0264 334614	*			*		Business as usual.
LOMBARD NORTH CENTRAL	Lombard House, 3 Princess Way, Redhill, Surrey RH1 1NK T 0737 774111 F 0737 778977				*		Existing customers only.
ROYSCOT TRUST LTD	Royscot House, The Promenade, Cheltenham, Glos. GL50 1PL T 0242 224455 F 0242 263861				*		Actively considering good commercial mortgages.
SCOTTISH AGRICULTURAL SECURITIES CORP. PLC	19 Rutland Square, Edinburgh EH1 2BA T 031 225 5829 F 031 220 2912	*			*		Business as usual.
INSURANCE COMPANIES							
ALLIED DUNBAR PROVIDENT PLC	9-15 Sackville Street, London W1A 2JF T 071 434 3211 F 071 437 9527	*					Investment property and professionals.
CENTURY LIFE PLC	5 Old Bailey, London EC4M 7BA T 071 332 5000 F 071 332 5030				*		Wide range of commercial mortgages.
THE GENERAL PRACTICE FINANCE CORP LTD	PO Box 21, Surrey Street, Norwich NR1 3NJ T 0603 682988 F 0603 683374				*		Specialist lender to doctors and dentists.
NORWICH UNION	PO Box 21, Surrey Street, Norwich NR1 3NJ T 0603 682986 F 0603 683374	*					Professionals and investment property.
PRUDENTIAL	142 Holborn Bars, London EC1N 2NH T 071 548 3089 F 071 548 3419	*					Will consider a range of commercial mortgages.
SUN LIFE OF CANADA	Burden House, 15 Buckingham Street, London WC2N 6DU T 071 925 0050 F 071 930 5250				*		£350k min with life policies £1m-£10m norm. Most properties considered.

Exhibit 3.18

Exhibit 3.19

Comments from entrepreneurs
who have used VCR to raise capital

"The vital link between ideas and funds." **The Observer**
"The success rate is encouragingly high." **New Scientist**

"The introduction we had to VCR was one of the best things that has happened to us! The service was first rate throughout. Every care was taken by VCR to assure that the original article was accurate and complete, and the charges for successfully raising £350,000 were most reasonable."

Roy Martin (56) had nearly 30 years experience in marine salvage and was qualified as a Master Mariner. He founded Marine Salvage Services in 1989 and subsequently sought £350,000 for 49.5% of the equity to finance the recovery of cargoes of precious and non-ferrous metals off the south west coast of England and Brittany *(Marine Salvage,* VCR, November 1992).

"I had 12 serious approaches, 7 of these were within the first week of VCR being published. I was delighted to subsequently raise the £150,000 I sought from one of them. I had offers from individuals, a consortium of private investors, and a venture capital company, and was very fortunate to be able to choose the investor who best matched my management style. The VCR write-up also provided a very useful condensed business plan, and their guidance on how to structure the deal was invaluable."

Julia Woodham-Smith (31) had read classics at Oxford and had started up a mail order catalogue to sell classic traditional clothes from around the world. After three years, Wealth of Nations had sales of £206,000 and sought expansion capital of £150,000 and offered 20% of the equity. *(World Design Classics,* VCR, July 1992).

"I am pleased to recommend VCR as an efficient and cost-effective means of reaching prospective investors. Great care was taken to produce an accurate and informative write-up, which was completed speedily and professionally."

Tony Bonvolsin (61) was an officer in HM Customs & Excise before becoming a successful entrepreneur. He sought £200,000 for 35% of the equity to fund the expansion of Dartmoor Water Limited and their product, Devon Hills mineral water *(Pure Spring Water,* VCR, August 1992).

"As a young entrepreneur aged 22 I found it hard to get good advice. After 1/2 hour with VCR my venture had been thoroughly appraised and I knew precisely what I needed. Three weeks later, after publication in VCR, I had raised the full £250,000 I sought. That was 10 years ago, since then I have been back twice more. Each time I have been pleased to find that I have been given outstanding support at all stages of the process between entrepreneur and investor."

Ashley Dobbs (31) raised £250,000 through VCR in October 1983 to fund the successful conversion of Flanesford Priory into holiday cottages. He returned to VCR in 1992 to raise £1.2m for a joint development with the Prudential *(Village Development,* VCR, June 1992).

"When I needed to raise money, VCR were the obvious choice. They were both helpful and professional and the money was raised from a private investor in less than 30 days."

Ieuan Shute (42) had worked for major dairy producers before he founded Riversleigh Foods in 1990. He sought £30,000 to develop his small Dorset based yogurt manufacturing business and offered 37.5% of the equity *(Yogurt Manufacturer,* VCR, March 1992).

Venture Capital Report Ltd, Boston Road, Henley on Thames, Oxon RG9 1DY UK Tel (0491) 579999 Fax (0491) 579815

Exhibit 3.20

 **Venture Capital Report**

—Directly linking investors and entrepreneurs —

- est 1978 -

About VCR

"The report that 'inks the budding tycoon with investors." **Evening Standard**

"The report will remove some of the leg-work for investors who would often like to back small companies but can't afford the management time to go and look for them." **Financial Times**

VCR is an Associate Member of the British Venture Capital Association (BVCA)

VCR is the leading national Business Angel introduction agency, directly linking private investors and small businesses that have been appraised by VCR. VCR publishes a monthly Report which features details of small businesses seeking equity capital (£20,000-£2m) and is subscribed to by a network of predominantly private investors. Each Report features around 20 different projects, many of which have been appraised in a detailed five-page article written by VCR staff after reviewing a business plan and meeting the entrepreneurs concerned.

The articles written by VCR provide full details of the product and/or service, market and competition, comprehensive CVs of the entrepreneurs, photographs, financial data and a suggested financial structure, and the entrepreneur's full contact address.

Investors, increasingly referred to as **Business Angels,** subscribe annually to VCR to receive a regular flow of vetted, equity investment opportunities. VCR is also a source of joint venture and new product/technology development opportunities. VCR's 600+ subscribers are the largest group of active Business Angels in the UK, and consist of:

High Net Worth Individuals... 54%
Managing Directors of Private Companies...................... 28%
Financial Institutions and Others................................... 14%
Quoted Companies............. .... 4%

The VCR article format enables investors to make quick, informed decisions and to make direct, confidential contact with the entrepreneur.. A one year subscription to VCR costs £350 by cheque, or £300 by annual banker's order or credit card. (A **free trial subscription** provides two consecutive issues free of charge, if, in accordance with the Financial Services Act, a post-dated banker's order or credit card charge authority is signed; it can be cancelled at any time during the trial period).

Entrepreneurs seeking equity capital and/or partners for their businesses use VCR to present their propositions directly to a highly targeted group of investors, who may also have relevant expertise and resources to offer. Entrepreneurs interested in being written up first submit their business plan, or equivalent, for VCR to review. A member of VCR's staff then meets the entrepreneur at length, offers guidance and writes an article to be featured in one issue of the Report. A fee of £350 is charged if the proposition is written up and published. Entrepreneurs who successfully raise funds from VCR subscribers are charged a success fee of £1,000 + 2.5% of funds raised (not exceeding 5% of the total raised).

Advertisements and **loose leaf inserts** are also featured in the Report. These are written by entrepreneurs and by companies advertising their services. Advertisers are not required to meet
VCR staff nor to make full disclosure of information. The copy deadline for advertisements is the 20th of the month preceding publication, and for one-page loose-leaf inserts the 30th. The cost is £250 for an A4 page and **no** further success fee is charged if capital is raised.

A feature of general interest written by an expert in their field is included as a mid-page article in the Report each month.

VCR also publishes *The Venture Capital Guide to Venture Capital in the UK and Europe,* the most comprehensive guide on how and where to raise risk capital. Entrepreneurs and their financial advisers use it to identify suitable venture capital companies, and venture capitalists use it to keep abreast of competitors' portfolios. The Guide provides comprehensive details of over 1000 sources of capital, including the actual investments made by venture capital companies and CVs of their key executives. (6th ed hardback, 1,184 pp, £106 inc p&p).

Venture Capital Report Ltd, Boston Rd, Henley on Thames, Oxon RG9 1DY, UK. Tel 0491 579999 Fax 0491 579825

Exhibit 3.21

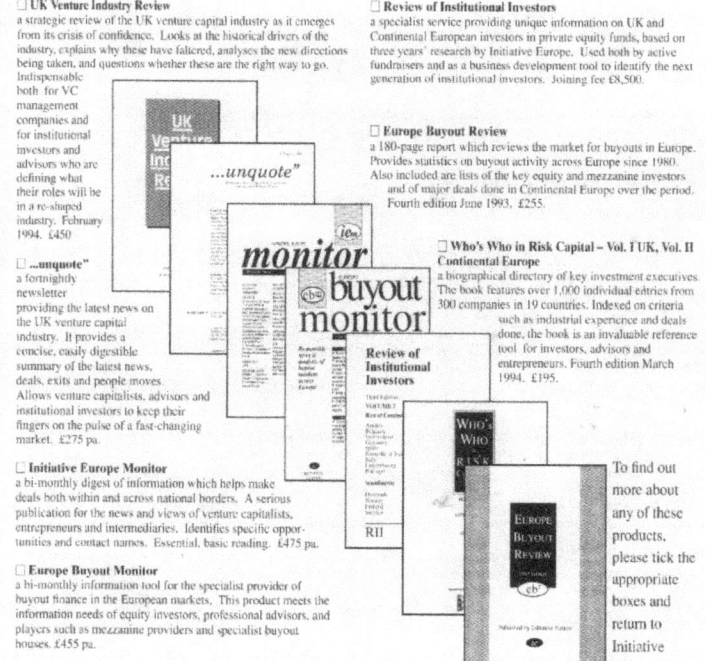

INITIATIVE EUROPE

INITIATIVE EUROPE was formed in 1988 to provide timely and accurate information for professionals involved in Europe's venture capital and buyout markets. The founders formerly worked for Venture Economics and the team members have between them 20 years' experience of reporting on risk capital markets in Europe. Today, Initiative Europe's publications are read by the majority of venture capitalists and their advisors, both in the UK and across Europe.

In order to publish its range of specialist journals on the European risk capital markets, Initiative Europe combines the most comprehensive database of relevant information - and direct access to its sources - with a unique facility to digest the information into formats which meet the identified needs of key players in the markets. Access to this unique resource is available exclusively by subscription to one or more of Initiative Europe's products, detailed below.

☐ UK Venture Industry Review
a strategic review of the UK venture capital industry as it emerges from its crisis of confidence. Looks at the historical drivers of the industry, explains why these have faltered, analyses the new directions being taken, and questions whether these are the right way to go. Indispensable both for VC management companies and for institutional investors and advisors who are defining what their roles will be in a re-shaped industry. February 1994. £450

☐ ...unquote"
a fortnightly newsletter providing the latest news on the UK venture capital industry. It provides a concise, easily digestible summary of the latest news, deals, exits and people moves. Allows venture capitalists, advisors and institutional investors to keep their fingers on the pulse of a fast-changing market. £275 pa.

☐ Initiative Europe Monitor
a bi-monthly digest of information which helps make deals both within and across national borders. A serious publication for the news and views of venture capitalists, entrepreneurs and intermediaries. Identifies specific opportunities and contact names. Essential, basic reading. £475 pa.

☐ Europe Buyout Monitor
a bi-monthly information tool for the specialist provider of buyout finance in the European markets. This product meets the information needs of equity investors, professional advisors, and players such as mezzanine providers and specialist buyout houses. £455 pa.

☐ Review of Institutional Investors
a specialist service providing unique information on UK and Continental European investors in private equity funds, based on three years' research by Initiative Europe. Used both by active fundraisers and as a business development tool to identify the next generation of institutional investors. Joining fee £8,500.

☐ Europe Buyout Review
a 180-page report which reviews the market for buyouts in Europe. Provides statistics on buyout activity across Europe since 1980. Also included are lists of the key equity and mezzanine investors and of major deals done in Continental Europe over the period. Fourth edition June 1993. £255.

☐ Who's Who in Risk Capital – Vol. I UK, Vol. II Continental Europe
a biographical directory of key investment executives. The book features over 1,000 individual entries from 300 companies in 19 countries. Indexed on criteria such as industrial experience and deals done, the book is an invaluable reference tool for investors, advisors and entrepreneurs. Fourth edition March 1994. £195.

To find out more about any of these products, please tick the appropriate boxes and return to Initiative Europe.

EUROPE'S PRIVATE EQUITY INFORMATION SPECIALISTS

INITIATIVE EUROPE

69 BONDWAY, LONDON SW8 1SQ. TEL: +44 71 735 9838. FAX: +44 71 820 0802

Exhibit 3.22

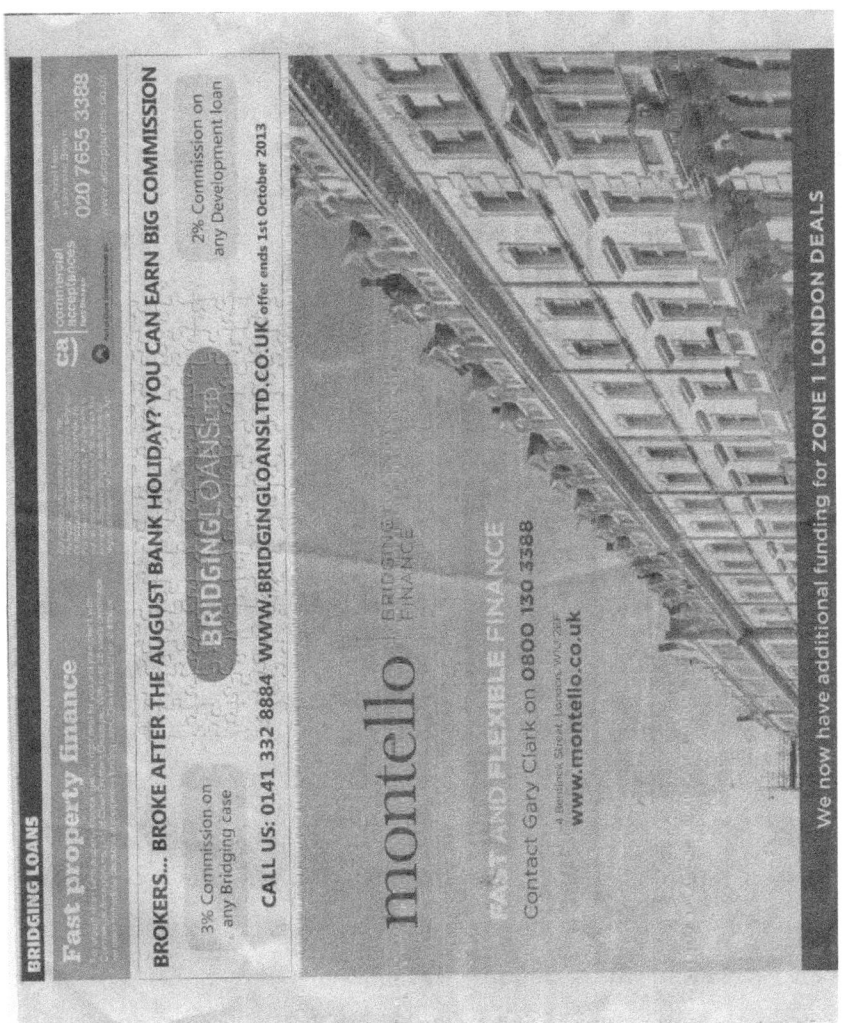

ABOUT THE AUTHOR
Ray Fox

Ray Fox is sixty-one years of age. He originally qualified with a B.Sc. (Hons.) degree in Behavioural Science (specialising in Industrial Psychology and Human Behaviour) from the University of Aston in Birmingham.

After graduation, he studied for and completed the examinations for The Institute of Chartered Secretaries and Administrators. He is a Fellow of the Institute (FCIS). Following that, he studied for and obtained a Diploma in Company Law and a Diploma in Company Secretarial Practice from the School of Accountancy and Business Studies.

For eight and a half years [from 1979 until 1987], Ray was the Company Secretary of a £50m turnover engineering company. In 1987 he joined Dun & Bradstreet, a US$3B turnover company, as their UK Company Secretary. Over the subsequent seven years, he was promoted to Company Secretary of D & B Europe, then the D & B Group and was subsequently appointed as their UK Director of Legal and Pensions Services. He was also Company Secretary of D & B Group's Pension Plan responsible for all administration and £100M of Pension Fund investments. Ray left D & B in 1994 to set up his own Consulting Practice.

For over twenty years, he has been running a very successful marketing consultancy specialising in the Legal profession. To date, he has worked with over 685 Solicitors' Practices, Law Firms, Patent Agents and Licensed Conveyancers, both in the UK and overseas. His support for the Legal profession has tended to fall into one of four broad categories:

1. Helping them generate more Clients

2. Helping them sell, merge or value their Practices

3. Helping them acquire other Practices

4. Helping them with P I insurance and staff recruitment

He has worked for over 300 Solicitors' practices helping them generate more Commercial Clients.

In addition to the above, he is one of the Founder Members and a Director of Core Legal, [see www.CoreLegal.net] which is a networking organisation of professional companies all of whom provide specialist support to the legal profession. He was also a General Commissioner of Taxes and one of the Co-Authors of "Running a Successful Law Firm – Strategies and Tips for Success".

He is active in Freemasonry, having been Worshipful Master of a number of Lodges and is also a member of The Worshipful Company of Chartered Secretaries and Administrators, one of the modern Livery Companies of the City of London.

Ray is also the brains behind a number of highly successful web sites:

www.BottomLineConsultancy.com

www.SolicitorSupermarket.biz

www.RecruitmentForSolicitors.co.uk

www.NEDexchange.co.uk

www.ProfessionalDirectors.co.uk

www.YourEnglishOffice.com

www.YourAmericanOffice.biz

www.TradeAndFinanceDiploma.com

www.StopTheTaxMan.com

www.WorldMoneyExchange.co.uk

www.Estelle-Alan-Group.com

www.EstelleAlanPublications.com

www.CompanyFormationCorporation.com

www.InsuranceForSolicitors.co.uk

www.UKTradeAdvisoryServices.com

www.YourOffshoreBankAccount.biz

OTHER BOOKS BY THE AUTHOR

More Commercial Clients And How To Get Them

A 'How To' Book for Solicitors' Practices
Published: 2014

ISBN: 978-1505488715

I know we don't want to admit it or say the words out loud but here goes – "Generally, Solicitors are crap at marketing". There, I've said it. We all know it's true but what can we do about it? A lot of Solicitors Practices will spend a lot of money on marketing, but this doesn't often pick up more commercial clients - a group who are often more profitable than a typical private client. This book is about how to get more commercial clients.

How To Make £1000 Per Week Running Your Own Import / Export Agency

Published: 2015

ISBN: 978-1507722176

Have you ever thought about running your own import / export business? Do you want to know what to do and how to go about it? This handy little book contains tips, the steps, letter and agency

contract templates, which you can amend and use for your own purpose. It is absolutely possible to make £1,000 Per Week Running Your Own Import / Export Agency from home.

How To Make £1,000 Per Week Running Your Own Unique Marketing Business

Published: 2015

ISBN: 978-1511693912

Would you like to operate and grow a business working from home? This book explains how you can start your own unique marketing business - working from home, and make up to £1,000 per week doing so.

Running A Successful Law Firm

Strategies & Tips for Success
Published: 2014

ISBN: 978-1492870890

Corelegal specialise in working with solicitors / lawyers. Between the contributing authors there is over 100 years collective experience. This book aims to bring that knowledge to you – giving you

fresh ideas and perspective. Avoid the expensive, painful and time consuming mistakes that most solicitors make and make your law firm a profitable success!

OTHER BOOKS WHICH MIGHT BE OF INTEREST

Constant Cashflow
How to Make Money Flow To You Every Single Day
Published: 2014

ISBN: 978-1 500601225

The problem with 'Cashflow' is that often businesses and individuals are too reliant on just one income stream/ source. Instead of just having 'one/two' jobs or key clients, and 'twenty' expenses, why not turn this around? What this book promotes is that everyday should be a payday - and it explains how and why.

Make The Most of Your Money
How to budget, save and manage your finances.
First Published: 2013

ISBN: 978-1481990639

This book looks at how to make the most of your money. Often the harder you work, the less you have to show for it. This book covers the issue of money. All the stuff you should have been taught in school including income, stocks, bonds, assets, reducing debt, mortgages, loans.

How To Write A Book In Two Weeks (or Less)

First Published: 2013

ISBN: 978-1492273554

Do you have a burning desire to write a book, but don't know how? Have you been thinking about writing a book for a while, but have just never 'gotten round to it?' Would you like to get your book completed quickly? Serial entrepreneur & author Lisa Newton explains how to write a book in two weeks (or less), which works particularly well for writing non-fiction books, business books and self-help books.

Think And Grow Rich

First Published: 2015

ISBN: 978-1505889352

Originally published in 1937, Napoleon Hill interviewed over 500 of the most affluent men and women of his time, and documented their secrets to wealth. Fast forward to present day and business people, top achievers and entrepreneurs alike still refer to this timeless classic. The money-making instructions that Hill outlines are just as powerful today as they were when first written. This exciting updated and revised edition by serial author and entrepreneur Lisa Newton expands on Hill's work and can be used as a workbook.

To order further copies of this book please fill in the form:

No. of copies	Title	Price	Total
	More Commercial Clients And How To Get Them	£12.50	
	How To Make £1,000 Per Week Running Your Own Import /Export Agency	£10.00	
	How To Make £1000 Per Week Running Your Own Unique Marketing Business	£10.00	
	How To Make £25k-£100k In Your Own Venture Capital Business	£10.00	
	For P&P add **£2.50** for the first book, **£1** for each extra book		
	GRAND TOTAL		**£**

Name: _____

Address: _____

City: _____ Country: _____

Postcode / Zip: _____

Daytime Tel. No./Email: _____

(in case of query)

I enclose a Cheque made payable to **The Bottom Line Consultancy** for £
_____

Please return forms to: (Photocopies acceptable)
Direct Mail Dept., The Bottom Line Consultancy, Hurst Cottage, Bottle Square Lane, Radnage, Buckinghamshire. HP14 4DP, UK
Enquiries to: fox@estelle-alan.com

The Bottomline Consultancy (directly or via its agents) may mail, email or phone you about promotions or products. [ ] Tick box if you do not want these from us
www.BottomLineConsultancy.com

www.ingramcontent.com/pod-product-compliance
Lightning Source LLC
Chambersburg PA
CBHW071002180526
45168CB00003B/1248